SKI IN SIX DAYS

Billy Kidd

with Douglas Kent Hall

Henry Regnery Company · Chicago

Published by Henry Regnery Company
            180 North Michigan Avenue
            Chicago, Illinois 60601
Manufactured in the United States of America
Library of Congress Catalog Card Number: 75-14246
International Standard Book Number: 0-8092-8310-7 (cloth)
                              0-8092-8309-3 (paper)

Published simultaneously in Canada by
Fitzhenry & Whiteside Limited
150 Lesmill Road
Don Mills, Ontario M3B 2T5
Canada

contents

	introduction	1
chapter one	before you start	2
chapter two	day one	14
chapter three	day two	38
chapter four	day three	50
chapter five	day four	70
chapter six	day five	76
chapter seven	day six	86
	glossary	99
	index	103

introduction

I have taken my experience of twenty-five years on skis and the principles of racing technique, especially of the racing turn, and have worked them into the basic materials for what I feel is a straightforward, no-nonsense approach to learning how to ski. I believe I can help you learn the basics of this sport in six days. By the end of that time, you ought to be able to make a parallel turn and be proficient enough to ski fifty percent of the trails in the United States.

In racing, the demands were great and the risks were high. I had to handle a combination of high speeds, varied terrain, and changing snow conditions; I had to make between 100 and 400 turns per race. The loss of a hundredth of a second on each turn could have cost me the race. Also, needless expenditure of energy would have increased my chances of getting tired, which would have left me open to injury. It became essential that I fully understand everything I could expect from myself and my skis and develop a technique that was simple and efficient. These have become the two most important concepts in my approach to skiing and to teaching people how to ski.

I found I could use the same principles I employed in perfecting my technique as a racer to teach a beginner to ski confidently and well in a very short time. These principles became the foundation for my teaching method, and they are the basis of this book. My method is simple but thorough. I have put together a body of instructional material that covers all the basic facets of skiing technique. This is a short course, but it is a sensible one.

Billy Kidd

1

chapter one

Skiing is not nearly as complicated or difficult as it may appear to someone who has never tried it. The sport consists of only a few basic maneuvers that can be mastered with as little as six days of practice. And even the practicing one has to do to be a proficient skier can be a lot of fun. Any skier, whether on a beginning slope or on the most complicated runs, experiences the thrill of moving quickly across the snow and the excitement of being able to complete a run.

What makes skiing appear complicated, and what, in fact, adds both to the difficulty of learning the sport and to the fun of doing it, is the speed at which a skier moves. The skier must know what to do — how to move, how to go into a turn and come out of one, when and how to slow down or speed up, and, most importantly, how to

before you start

look and plan ahead. This is as important for the safety of you and everyone else on the slopes as it is for the pleasure you can have. The more you know about skiing well, the more fun you will have and the greater your sense of accomplishment will be.

But first, any skier must be in at least reasonably good physical condition and must be properly equipped. Skis, boots, bindings, poles, clothing, and lifts and tows may appear to be strange, cumbersome, and complicated to the beginner. But there is nothing about this equipment that cannot be understood as well by the beginner as by the champion skier. To make your first and every experience on the ski slopes exciting and rewarding, you would be wise to learn a little about yourself and about the equipment you will be using.

3

GETTING INTO SHAPE

It is entirely conceivable that you could come to skiing without being in good physical condition. Persons who work out regularly should not be concerned about needing any additional conditioning before skiing. But, those who do not get much exercise will find skiing easier, safer, and, probably, far more enjoyable in the long run if they make some special effort to prepare themselves.

Sporting Lifestyle

There are a number of ways you can get into shape — all good, all readily available in most areas. Yoga exercise programs are desirable for skiers because they promote stretching and relaxing of the muscles and good breathing habits in addition to balance and coordination. Participating in tennis, biking, handball, swimming, basketball, volleyball, or jogging will also effectively prepare your body for skiing. I feel, however, that jogging has a drawback. It does little to promote coordination of the eyes and feet. This can be overcome simply by jogging in the woods or in some other varied terrain where you will have to be concerned with concentration and balance.

There are also a number of things you can do in your everyday life that will improve your condition and help make you more aware of your body. Walk when you could ride. Walk up stairs instead of taking an elevator. Take stairs two at a time. One of the best all around exercises that takes very little time, equipment, or space is jumping rope. It builds the arms, lungs, thighs, ankles, and feet, as well as good coordination.

However you choose to get in shape, there are three goals you should try to achieve. Develop your general physical strength, concentrating on your legs, arms, back and stomach — roughly in that order. Build up your breathing power in order to cope with skiing at high altitudes. And work at loosening up your body, because, especially in the beginning, you will be falling a lot and, if you are stiff, your chances for injury are greater.

Warm-up Exercises

In addition to the help that other sports and the things you can do

Billy Kidd and Doug Hall are ready to ski.

every day can give toward getting you into shape, a short series of warm-up exercises will help loosen up your body and prepare you for the day on skis. These seven exercises work in a logical progression from the head down to the feet that is symbolic of a lot of what I will be saying about skiing. I would like you always to start with your head, in the sense that you think through an exercise before you go ahead with it. These exercises should serve to remind you of three words that are the keys to good, safe skiing: THINK, RELAX, FEEL.

None of the exercises will be strenuous. You should not hurry through them. Be slow and methodical. Think about them. Relax. And feel what they do to your body. The main idea here is to stretch your muscles and help you loosen up.

Plan to spend about five minutes doing these exercises each morning. Do them before you eat or drink. And wear loose, comfortable clothing — no shoes or belts or other tight-fitting articles.

1. Rolling Your Head. Stand with your feet a few inches apart and place your hands on your hips. Relax. Let your head drop until your chin rests on your chest. Now roll your head slowly to the left, letting it go all the way around until it returns to the first position on your chest. You should imagine yourself making a complete circle with your head. Repeat the exercise two more times, *slowly,* to the left. As you roll your head, you should feel the muscles pull in your neck and a gentle loosening sensation in your spine. Now repeat the exercise three times more, but make your circles *slowly* to the right. Pause before going to the next exercise.

2. Swinging Your Arms. Stand comfortably, with your feet slightly apart. Relax. Swing your left arm in a circle parallel to your body. (If you were holding a bucket full of water it would go over your head without spilling.) Start slowly, feeling your arm and shoulder muscles stretch and pull, and increase the speed of the circles until your arm is going around at a moderate speed. Not too fast. The rest of your body should remain as relaxed as possible. Now, still with your left arm, reverse the direction of the circle; start slowly and increase the speed. Pause for a moment and then do the same exercise with your right arm. Stop and relax completely.

3. Circling with Your Hips. Stand with your feet a few inches apart and your hands on your hips. Throw your hips forward so you feel your body arch. Now move *slowly* to the left, making a circle with your hips. As you push your hips forward, you should feel your stomach muscles stretch. While moving to the sides, you should feel the muscles stretch and pull from your rib cage to your hips. And as you get to the back of the circle you should feel the pull of the muscles in your back and in the backs of your legs. Do this exercise three times to the left and three times to the right. Remember that it will be most effective if you do it slowly and with control. Again, pause briefly before going on to the next exercise.

4. Touching Your Toes. Stand with your feet a few inches apart, your arms at your sides, and the rest of your body relaxed. Starting slowly, bend as far as gravity takes you, until you start to feel the muscles pull in the backs of your legs. Relax briefly. Let gravity pull you down a little farther, then a little farther. The object of this exercise is not to touch your toes but to stretch your muscles and help you relax. If you attempt to force yourself, you will only do harm to your muscles. Many people are able to touch their toes immediately; others need a few days to limber up. However far you can bend, you should feel your hamstring muscles tighten first, then your back muscles. Do this exercise three times from the full, upright position, keeping your legs straight and bending slowly. Pause a moment before continuing.

5. Stretching Your Thigh Muscles. Stand with your feet spread about three feet. Place your hands on your knees. Lean *slowly* to the left, bending your left knee and keeping your right leg straight. You should feel the muscles stretch along the inside of your right leg and up into your groin. Now come back *slowly* to the beginning position. Lean *slowly* to the right. You should feel the muscles stretch along the inside of your left leg and up into your groin. Do this exercise three times to each side, alternating from left to right. Stand up, pause, and relax.

7

6. *Half Knee Bends to the Side. Special care should be taken while doing this exercise. It is extremely important to the skier. Doing it, you will assume a position similar to the one you use when you are skiing.* Stand with your feet a few inches apart and your hands on your hips. Keep your feet flat on the floor and do the movements of this exercise *slowly.* As you bend your knees forward — going down into a half knee bend position — bend them to the left. Your movement should be slow and smooth. Come back to a standing position and bend your knees forward and to the right. You should feel the muscles stretching in your thighs and the ligaments working in your knees. Repeat this exercise — *slowly, smoothly* — three times to each side. Relax with your arms loosely at your sides.

7. *Rolling Your Ankles.* Sit in a chair or on the edge of your bed. Cross your legs, placing your left foot just across your right knee. Take hold of your left foot and let it relax. Twist your left foot in slow gentle circles in a clockwise and counter-clockwise direction. The object of this exercise is to loosen the muscles and ligaments in your ankle and foot. Repeat the exercise for the right foot.

In all the conditioning you do, remember to work slowly. Push yourself but don't overdo. This is the same advice I will give you on the hill with your skis. The challenge you give yourself should be tempered with reason.

EQUIPMENT

In the beginning, while you are learning to ski, I suggest that you rent your equipment. This will give you a chance to try out various skis, boots, bindings, and poles, You will be able to familiarize yourself with the qualities and characteristics of the equipment you use, so that when you go to buy your own you will be able to make a knowledgeable decision about what you want and need.

You can rent equipment from a good ski shop near you and thus be assured of getting the kind of equipment you want to use. Or you can rent it at the ski area, the advantage being that you can correct any problems with equipment that arise when you get on the hill.

Skis

When beginning skiing, most people ought to use short skis. This is another good reason for renting your equipment. Skis are measured in centimeters (cm). Persons of average height should use 150-cm skis (approximately five feet long). If you are less than about five and a half feet tall, or if you are timid, you can use 140-cm skis.

Boots

Fit is the most important consideration in choosing boots. You should try boots on with two or three pairs of medium thickness socks. (Several pairs of medium-weight socks are preferable to one pair of heavy, bulky socks.) Wear the boots around the shop for ten or fifteen minutes to make sure there are no pressure points. They should be well padded around the tops and they should be resilient enough that when they are buckled you can bend your knees forward three or four inches.

Bindings

The bindings are the set of fastenings that hold the boots firmly onto the skis. They release your ski whenever too much pressure is put on the mechanism. They should be adjusted in the shop according to your weight and skiing ability. Make sure that you understand how they work, that you see them release, and that you can get back into them easily. Ask for a demonstration of how to loosen and tighten them in case you should have to do this on the hill.

Poles

Ski poles are usually made of a lightweight metal with leather hand grips and wrist straps at one end and encircling disks called baskets placed a few inches above the points at the other ends. Your poles should be the proper length for your height. To determine this, place your elbow by your side while you grasp the pole—your forearm should be level.

Clothing

It is important to be comfortable when you ski. Whether you are or not will be determined at least partially by how you dress.

I am a strong advocate of long johns, especially thermal underwear. They keep you warm and give you an extra layer of protection, two important considerations when you dress for the ski slopes.

A lightweight turtleneck, which can be worn under another sweater, will keep your neck and throat warm. *Do not wear long flowing scarves or other frivolous articles of clothing that can get caught in the mechanisms of the lifts.*

When choosing your pants and parka, pay careful attention to fit. They need to be loose enough to allow unrestricted movement but snug enough not to be cumbersome. Modern ski clothing is designed to be functional. Stretch fabrics allow you to move easily; they are warm, light in weight, and can breathe, keeping you comfortable no matter how active you get. In addition, many are constructed with special stretch inserts at stress points and sewn with very durable seams.

For the sake of both warmth and safety, you ought to wear gloves or mittens at all times. Mittens are warmer than gloves, but it's easier to do such things as buckle your boots and put on safety straps with gloves. Today, thanks to better methods of contruction and insulation, gloves are almost as warm as mittens. Whichever you choose to wear, remember to keep them on as protection against possible frostbite and injury from falls.

Never go out on the slopes without sunglasses or specially designed ski goggles. At high altitudes the ultraviolet rays are extremely harmful to the eyes. Buy either shatterproof glass or plastic lenses for safety.

Almost everyone needs some kind of protection from the effects of sun and wind. Carry a sun block and wear suntan lotion or wind cream. It is best to tan slowly and remain comfortable.

One final word about ski clothing: Wear it in layers so you can take it off and put it on as the weather changes.

SKI AREAS

You're bound to feel a little awkward moving around an unfamiliar place in an unfamiliar way. It will help if you know something about the operations and procedures at a ski area.

Tows and Lifts

A few simple words of instruction and caution about tows and lifts, which carry skiers to the tops of the slopes, can save the beginner a lot of trouble and bother. There are several different basic designs that fulfill the specific needs of various areas and runs. The chairlift is probably the most convenient method of getting skiers to the top of a hill and probably — with the exception of the gondola — the easiest to use. You might encounter other types of lifts as well, so I am including a short discussion of the procedure to follow in using each kind of tow and lift.

Rope Tow. The rope tow is a long rope run on a system of pulleys that takes the skier — on his skis — to the top of the slope. It is simple to use, but it can be very tiring if you fight it. The mistake most beginners make is to grab the rope immediately. This can jerk you, throw you off balance, and cause you to fall. What you should do is let the rope slip freely through your hands at first and gradually tighten your grip until you start to move. Then increase the pressure of your grip until the rope is not slipping at all. Lean back, keeping your arms straight and your knees slightly bent to take the shock of acceleration and changes in terrain. In the event that you need to slow down or stop completely because of a pile-up, simply loosen your grip gradually, allowing the rope to slip through your hands. When the congestion clears, follow the same procedure you used at the bottom to resume your former speed.

Poma Lift. The poma lift consists of a pole with a small disk attached to the base. I suggest that, as with all the lifts, you take a few moments to watch experienced skiers get on before you make your initial trip. Then approach the lift with your poles held in the hand away from the operator. The operator will hand you the pole and disk. Put the disk between your legs and let it come to rest firmly behind your buttocks. *Do not sit on the disk.* The unit itself will accelerate in much the same fashion you might use on starting on the rope tow and will pull you along on your skis. When you arrive at

11

the unloading area, take hold of the pole firmly, let the disk slip from between your legs, and keep a gentle grip on the pole until it swings away and you can ski off to the side.

T-Bar and J-Bar Lifts. T-bar and J-bar lifts are poles suspended from cables that have either a T-shaped (for two skiers) or a J-shaped (for one skier) configuration at their base. Approach the T-bar lift holding your poles away from the lift. Wait until the skiers in front of you have been lifted away and then get quickly into position. The lift operator will place the bar firmly under your buttocks. You should take hold of the pole with your free hand. *Do not sit down.* Just relax and allow the lift to pull you to the top. To unload, push off gently and ski away from the path of the lift.

Chairlift. A chairlift looks something like a small porch swing suspended from a cable. Chairlifts are designed to transport one, two, or three people; the most commonly used is the double chairlift. Before you get on a chairlift watch a few people loading. Get into position, holding your poles in the hand away from the centerpole of the chairlift. The operator will bring the chair against the backs of your legs. *Sit down at once and lift up the tips of your skis.* Take care to keep your skis and poles safely away from the lift mechanism or from any objects you might pass on the way to the top. Sit back comfortably and do not attempt to swing the chair. The unloading procedure for the chairlift is similar to that for the T-bar. Holding your poles firmly in one hand, push away from the chair and ski off the ramp, continuing until you are safely out of the way.

Six Basic Rules for Using All Lifts

1.   Before riding any lift, read all the instructions for its use. They will be posted at the bottom of the hill and repeated along the way.

2.   Do not try to hurry in the line, and be considerate of fellow skiers waiting with you.

3.   Carry your poles firmly in one hand, the hand away from the operator or the support pole of the lift, *with the straps off your wrists.*

4. If you should fall as the lift starts, *do not try to hang on.* Let go, and fall away from the lift.

5. Keep your poles and other gear away from the mechanism of the lift and the other obstacles along its path.

6. Remember that there will be sufficient time for safe unloading at the top. Do not rush yourself, but do be prepared. Ski away as quickly and smoothly as possible, leaving the unloading area clear for the skiers behind you.

Ski Etiquette

Ski etiquette is based on logic and grounded in common sense and the basic rules of courtesy.

To begin with, you must always be in control of your skis. You should always be able to stop for or be able to miss other skiers or objects on the hill. This means you should only ski trails that are matched by your level of proficiency and always wear securely fastened safety straps to prevent runaway skis.

It is also very important to look out for other skiers because people traveling very quickly may not always be able to avoid you easily. Look uphill before starting down a trail or resuming your descent from a side. Never stop so that you block a trail or in a place where skiers coming down from above cannot see you in plenty of time to ski around you. After a fall, if it is at all possible, get to the side of the trail to keep from causing an accident. And never stop where you will make it difficult for skiers to unload safely from a lift.

When you are skiing downhill or overtaking another skier, you are responsible for avoiding the skier below you. If you are approaching another skier on an opposite traverse, you should pass each other on the right side.

Whenever you are walking or climbing on a ski area, you should be wearing your skis and you should keep to the side of the trail.

Familiarize yourself with the regulatory signs that pertain to the area you have chosen to ski. You can do this easily during your initial lift ride. Remember that there is always some good reason for an area being posted off limits. Pay attention to such signs and to all other traffic signs and you will be sure to have an exciting experience whenever you ski.

13

chapter two

Y ou have chosen to learn one of the most exciting and satisfying individual sports in the world. Unfortunately there is a great deal of misinformation about skiing. The truth is that from the very first day skiing can be simple, safe, and rewarding.

To become relatively proficient on skis, you need merely to acquaint yourself with a few basic principles and to learn to use some muscles you normally might not use. In today's lesson you will work mainly to develop your sense of balance and learn a few elementary techniques for controlling your skis. This should give you the self-confidence you need to find a harmony with the mountain and allow you to have your first real experiences in a challenging and exhilerating sport.

Do not buy a lift ticket today. You will not need one until you can

day one

stop and can turn in both directions. For your first lessons, you should be on a beginner's slope. All good ski areas have these special facilities for the beginning skier. If your area does not, get a trail map and choose a quiet, flat place away from the expert skiers, one with gentle slopes and flat outruns. Tie your skis firmly together with their safety straps to make a compact unit. Then you can carry them easily on your shoulder. Have you done the seven important warm-up exercises?

GETTING THE FEEL OF SKIS
Put on your skis on the flat at the bottom of the hill. Using a gloved hand or the tip of a pole, make sure the soles of your boots are free

If you tie your skis firmly together with their safety straps, you can carry them easily on your shoulder.

from snow so that they will fit into the bindings properly. Then fasten the safety straps so that their buckles are on the outside; this prevents them from catching and causing a fall.

A lot of people, even some who have skied for years, don't know how to put on their poles. This is unfortunate as the straps, which are designed to fit your wrist comfortably, will provide support when you are planting your poles or pushing with them. To put your poles on properly, first place your hands through the straps from the underside of the loop. Then bring your palms down on top of the straps and clasp the handles of the poles.

Exercises to Help You Adjust to Skis

To familiarize yourself with the new weight and extension on your feet, do the following exercises:

Stand balanced with your poles, lift one ski, point the tip down at the snow, and then turn it to the right and the left. Do the same with the other ski.

16

To put your poles on, first put your hand through the underside of the loop (above left); then bring your palm down on top of the strap and clasp the handle of the pole (above right).

One exercise to familiarize yourself with the feel of skis is to roll each ski from one edge to the other just by moving your knee from side to side.

In the basic ski position, your body should be as follows: feet three or four inches apart, knees bent, hips directly over your feet, and torso bent slightly at the waist with rounded back and shoulders.

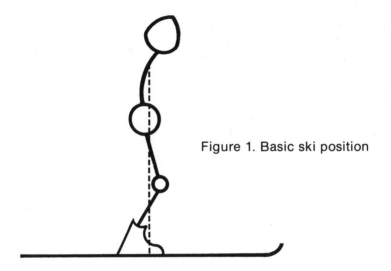

Figure 1. Basic ski position

Now slide one ski forward and backward, using only your leg muscles. Slide the other ski.

Now, while your ski is flat on the snow, roll it from one edge to the other by just moving your knee from side to side until it feels comfortable. Do the same with the other ski. *Your knee will bend sideways easily if it is also bent forward slightly.*

The Basic Ski Position

The basic athletic position is what all other positions in a sport build from. It allows the feet, knees, hips, shoulders, hands, and head to interact with each other in the fastest and most efficient way. To assume the basic athletic position for skiing, I suggest starting with your feet and working upward to your head. Place your feet three or four inches apart, which is roughly the same distance apart as your hips and shoulders are. Bend your knees forward until you feel your shins resting gently against the fronts of your boots. (If your ankles feel too confined and uncomfortable, loosen the top buckles of your boots.) Keep your hips directly over your feet. Bend slightly at the waist and round your back and shoulders.

Your back should form one continuous C-shaped curve from

your hips to your shoulders — instead of the natural S-shaped curve it has when you are standing upright. Your arms should be relaxed, elbows bent slightly away from your body; your hands should be waist high and forward.

This basic athletic position, or basic ski position, should leave you relaxed. It should help you keep your weight over the balls of your feet, give you a wide enough stance for good balance, and keep your whole body ready to react instantly to any changes in motion and terrain that you encounter.

MOVING ON SKIS

Walking

To further familiarize yourself with the sensation of wearing skis, you need to practice walking. Walk as you would normally, sliding your skis instead of lifting them up off the snow. Feel what happens to your body, especially to your ankles and knees. Pay attention to the way your skis respond to your weight and how you must exaggerate in order to walk smoothly. *If you push very gently your ski will not slip backward.*

When you are comfortable walking on skis alone, use your poles to help. Plant your poles in the snow, moving them in unison with the opposite ski — right pole — left ski; left pole — right ski. Keep your poles angled back. Establish a definite rhythm between your skis and poles. Use your upper arms to push forward on your poles.

Now try propelling yourself farther by pushing with both poles in unison. As you do this, note how your body drops into position — down and slightly forward. Keep it relaxed. This is very important.

Looking Ahead

You should always look ahead instead of down at your body or your skis. This will help your concentration and your balance. It also

(Facing page) To walk when wearing skis, move as you would normally but slide your skis instead of lifting them from the snow.

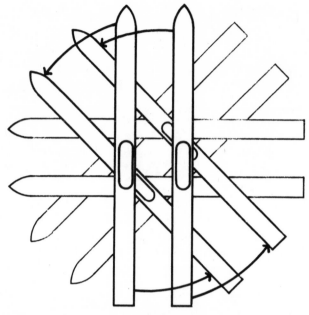

Figure 2. Turn by rotating both tips and tails of your skis.

prepares you for any upcoming changes in terrain and contributes to maintaining a good upright body position. It may sound strange for me to be telling you to look where you are going, but my experience is that far too many beginners get too involved in watching their skis and forget to pay attention to the direction in which they are traveling. So let me emphasize this point: *Part of good, confident skiing is looking ahead and knowing where you are going.*

Turning

As a preliminary exercise that will give you more practice manipulating your skis, walk in large circles and figure eights. Be certain you are in the basic athletic position. This will make your movements easier and more liquid.

When you are comfortable with the preliminary exercise, practice turning around completely by rotating the tips and tails of your skis around your feet. Make your steps small and rhythmical. This may

One way to climb a hill on skis is to step up it sideways, using the ski edges (right) as they bite into the snow to avoid slipping downhill.

seem awkward at first, and you will probably find yourself stepping on your skis, but after a short practice period you ought to feel your control increasing.

This is the first introduction to rotating your skis around your feet, one of the principal parts of the modern ski turn. From this you learn how to steer your skis into a turn.

Climbing Side Step

To learn the climbing side step, choose a short, gentle incline that is out of the way of all traffic. Keeping your skis horizontal to the fall line (the path a snowball rolling down the hill would take) step sideways up the hill. To avoid sliding downhill, make the edges of your skis bite into the snow by bending your knees in toward the hill. To avoid sliding forward or backward, keep your skis at absolute right angles to the fall line.

Now practice this exercise *without* the use of your poles. Concentrate on rhythm and balance. Pause and note what is happening to your legs. You should be able to feel the effects of the stretching and pulling of your muscles.

To get the full benefit of this exercise, alternate positions on the hill. Climb with left ski uphill for a while; then climb with the right ski uphill.

During my early years of training to be a racer in Stowe, Vermont, when I was trying to make the basics of skiing automatic, I would purposely sidestep up a slalom course instead of taking the lift. It wasn't the easiest way, of course, but I knew it would help me become a better skier. Basically, sidestepping helped me build up the muscles in my legs and taught me to roll my knees into the hill to edge my skis and to keep the rest of my weight balanced over my feet.

Straight Running

Find a gentle slope with a flat outrun or a slightly uphill outrun. There should be no obstacles. Climb to the top of the slope and make the following preparations for your first downhill run:

1. Stand with your skis placed horizontally across the slope and your upper body turned and facing downhill. Plant your poles below your skis a shoulders' width apart. Lean on your poles, with your arms outstretched to support your body.

2. Taking small careful steps, rotate your skis around until they are parallel to the fall line and spaced a few inches apart.

3. Your body should be in the basic ski position— ankles and knees bent forward, back slightly rounded. Your weight should be on the balls of your feet and equally distributed on both of your skis. You are now ready to begin your descent.

4. To start your first run, lift your poles and hold them just

Getting ready and then letting go for a
straight run

slightly away from your body; bend your elbows to keep the baskets on the poles back and out of the snow.

5. Remain relaxed and look ahead. Watch where you are going! Keep your knees bent and relaxed to absorb any changes in terrain (you should be aware of these changes through your feet).

After a few runs, try lifting the tail of each ski in turn to shift your weight to the other ski. Notice how the weighted ski reacts in the snow.

Once you have made a straight run, you have skied. I remember my own first time. I was five years old, and I had new wood skis. It was a big moment in my life. My father was filming the event with his movie camera. I only went about twenty feet before I lost my balance and fell over backwards. But I remember lying there in the snow with a big grin on my face and thinking, "I'm a skier!" That did it. I was hooked on skiing.

Even now, when my family gets together to laugh at these old

If a fall is inevitable, fall to the side. To get up, slide your skis downhill from your body and position them horizontally across the fall line.

Use your poles in the manner shown to help yourself stand up.

films, I can see why I fell backwards. I hadn't yet learned one simple rule: Keep your knees bent forward.

The fact that I notice my mistake in the film gives the story a further significance. An invaluable aid to understanding what you are doing right and what mistakes you are making is to have a friend take still pictures or movies of you on skis. You can study these pictures at home, make note of any problems you might be having, and correct them the next time you are on skis.

Falling

If you feel a fall is inevitable, it is better to fall to the side, keeping your skis and legs parallel and your poles out to the side. Remain relaxed and do not fight the fall.

The easiest way to get up is to slide your skis downhill from your body and position them horizontally across the fall line. If one or both of your bindings have released, wait until you are standing to refasten them. *If possible, edge over to the side of the slope, out of the way of any oncoming skiers.*

Pull your skis up close to your body to give yourself some leverage while standing up. Plant your poles together above the skis and near your hips. With your uphill hand grip both poles just above the baskets and place your other hand on the tops of the poles. Then push your weight over your feet and stand up.

If a ski has come off and you have trouble keeping it from sliding downhill, place one of your gloves under it until you have your boot securely locked into the binding.

SNOWPLOW

The snowplow is a learning device to introduce you to the basic principles of skiing. It gives you a wider base so that you'll be less likely to fall at first. It is the key to control. It teaches you to edge your skis with a minimum of movement away from the basic ski position. In the snowplow you simply have to move your knees to edge your skis. The snowplow can teach you to rotate or steer your skis around your feet, which is the modern way of turning. The snowplow also forces you to exercise equally the muscles on both sides of your body so that you'll end up with two strong turns instead of one that is strong and one that is weak and dangerous.

Let me emphasize that the snowplow is a beginning exercise, but it is a very important one. (I still use the snowplow occasionally to slow down on narrow trails.) Practice it until you are comfortable with balance and edging. Then go on to the more advanced positions.

Basic Snowplow Procedure

Practice the snowplow position while stationary on the flat. Take the following steps:

1. Push the tails of your skis about a pole's length apart and keep the tips about three or four inches apart — forming a V. Be sure to bend your knees forward, round your back, and keep your hands forward.

2. Roll your knees to the inside and then to the outside of your skis to feel the action of edging. You should see the edges of

28

day one

Snowplow position from front and side

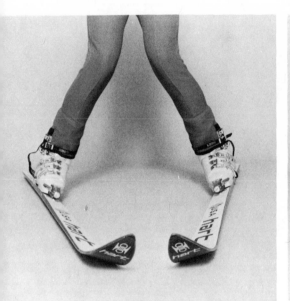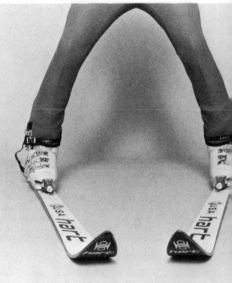

To get the feeling of edging, roll your knees to the inside (above left) and then to the outside (above right) of your skis.

your skis bite when you roll your knees in and see that your skis start to slide apart when you roll your knees out and flatten the skis.

3.   Now climb to the top of the slope. Get into the snowplow position by supporting yourself on your poles as you did in straight running, with your weight distributed evenly on both skis. Pull your poles out of the snow and let yourself start moving. Maintain your V-shaped plow by keeping the tails of your skis pushed away from you and the tips together. Remember that your knees should be bent and remain flexible.

To go slower, push the tails of your skis away from you and edge more by rolling your knees in. To go faster, flatten your skis and allow them to come closer, forming a smaller V. Practice these variations of the snowplow until you understand completely what the changes in the position of your skis are doing. You should now feel your first real sense of being able to control your skis.

Get into the snow-
plow position, sup-
porting yourself with
your poles, and then
pull your poles out of
the snow and let your-
self move downhill.

To slow yourself, push the tails of your skis away from you and edge your skis into the snow.

Snowplow and Straight Running

On the same slope where you learn the snowplow you can try combining the snowplow with straight running. Start at the top of the hill. Stand in a more upright position and release the edges of your skis. They will parallel naturally. Now lower your body again and push the tails of the skis away from you and into the snowplow position. Finish with a snowplow stop, which you can accomplish by pushing your skis apart and edging them more aggressively.

32

To go faster, flatten your skis and allow them to come closer together.

SNOWPLOW TURN

The snowplow position is the position from which the most elementary skiing turn is made.

Preturn Exercise

Practice the following movements on the flat at the bottom of the slope.

    1.   Assume the snowplow position on the flat.

2.   Increase the edging of your right ski by rolling your knee to the inside.

3.   Drop your right shoulder to put more weight on your right ski. Dropping your shoulder and rolling your knee inward should happen simultaneously. Take care that you don't twist your shoulder forward as you tilt it down. The combination of increased edging and increased weight on the right ski causes the ski to dig into the snow more and will turn you to the left.

4.   Return to the straight snowplow position.

5.   Now repeat the above maneuver to the other side: Left shoulder over left ski, left knee rolling inward to make a right turn.

Snowplow Turn

Climb to the top of the same gentle incline. Assume the snowplow position and start downhill. Keep your skis edged so that you are moving slowly and are in complete control. Simultaneously drop your right shoulder and roll your right knee in to edge your right ski. (Remember to keep your shoulders facing in the direction your skis are pointing.)

While you are still moving, try to steer both feet to the left. You should turn slightly to the left. Hold this snowplow-turn position until your skis turn 90 degrees and you are heading across the hill. You should come to a gradual stop.

Face downhill again and repeat the above movements to the opposite direction. Drop your left shoulder, roll your left knee in to edge and weight your left ski, and steer both feet simultaneously to the right. You will make a right turn and come to a stop.

CONCLUSION OF THE FIRST DAY

Detecting and Correcting Problems

One common mistake of beginning skiers is a tendency to sit back on their skis. If you are having this problem, the best way to correct it is to press your shins forward against the fronts of your boots.

In executing the preturn exercise turn to the left (top) and, after straightening (center), turn to the right (bottom). This exercise will help you understand the movements necessary to execute the snowplow turn.

Billy Kidd skis through a snow-plow turn and slides to a stop.

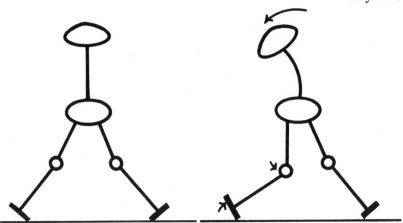

Figure 3. Changes in leg and body position in the snowplow turn

Another mistake you might be making is squatting down over your skis. If you are doing this, you are using much more energy to ski than you need and, consequently, you are tiring too quickly. To correct this, review the basic ski position, consciously standing upright and keeping your hips comfortably over your feet and your back only slightly rounded.

I would like to give you one final hint today. Your lesser weighted ski (the left ski in the left turn, or the right ski in the right turn) should be edged less than your weighted or turning ski. If this is giving you trouble, roll your knee out to flatten the unweighted ski and make it slide easily into the turn.

Review

Congratulations! During your first day on a slope you have learned how to control the direction of your skis, how to control your speed, and even how to turn. You have seen that the three basic principles of edging, weighting, and steering are all interrelated and relatively easy to learn. The experts, even the international competitors, use as the groundwork for their advanced techniques the three basics that you have learned in the first day. The rest of your skiing career will simply be to practice and refine these three basics by moving gradually up to increasingly more efficient and more graceful forms.

chapter three

As soon as you are awake, you should start thinking about skiing. Remember what it was like yesterday. Move your arms and legs and note which muscles you've been using. Do your warm-up exercises (see Chapter One) to work out the stiffness.

In your mind, as you are exercising, review what you learned yesterday. Form a mental picture of yourself on skis — *relaxed,* in the right position. Remember the feeling of being able to regulate your speed, of having enough control to turn and stop. Knowing these things should make you anxious to get your skis on and start a new day.

I cannot emphasize enough the value of taking these few moments to visualize yourself on skis. Mentally visualizing myself skiing has always been very helpful to me. I started working on this

day two

mental approach to my skiing almost ten years ago. From 1964 to 1969 I was a student at the University of Colorado and also a member of the U.S. Ski Team, both of which were full-time activities. I wanted to spend all my time racing, but I knew that I should go on and finish school. It was frustrating for me to know that my main rivals, Jean-Claude Killy and Karl Schranz, were out training while I was in the library studying. As a result, any time I had a few minutes away from my books I would think about skiing. I would analyze the racing turn and the body movements necessary to make it, and I would try to feel how it would be putting them into practice. I'd feel the fronts of my boots, the centrifugal force, and being balanced on my outside ski at the end of the turn. I fixed clearly in my mind what I wanted to do and then I visualized myself

Practice the snowplow position on the flat before you take the lift.

doing it. When I did get on the hill, which was about two days a week, everything seemed natural, and the improvements I was trying to make happened much faster than they ever had before.

Today you should buy a lift ticket. But plan to stay only on the beginners' hill, where the slopes are gentle and free from obstacles.

GETTING STARTED

Exercise on the Flat

Before taking the lift up the hill, stand on the flat and try the snowplow position as if you are going straight. Push your skis into a

40

On your first run today, practice slow,
easy snowplow turns. Stay relaxed and
feel what's happening.

V and bend your knees forward with your shins pressing against the
fronts of your boots. Position your hips directly over your feet and
round your back slightly to form a C with your backbone. Relax
your arms, keeping your elbows bent and your hands waist-high and
forward. Make sure your weight is distributed equally over the balls
of your feet and that your skis are edged equally, with your knees
rolled slightly inward. Focus your eyes ahead.

To simulate a left turn, drop your right shoulder and at the same
time roll your right knee inward to increase the edging of your
outside or right ski. Return to the center position. Now simulate a
right turn by edging and weighting your left ski.

First Run

For your first run, I suggest you do not take the lift. Climb part way up the hill. Climb for a while with your right ski uphill; then change and climb with your left ski uphill. This should help loosen up your muscles and give you some edging practice.

Pause before you begin your run and relax. Are you in the basic ski position? Do you feel comfortable? You are ready to begin.

Make several slow easy turns in each direction, steering your feet around while you drop your shoulder and roll your knee. Stay in each turn until you cross the fall line and come to a stop.

THE REST OF THE DAY

Riding the Lift

Once you have confidence in your ability to turn and come to a stop you are ready to ride the lift to the top of the beginners' hill. The lifts on beginners' hills are usually simple to ride and run very slowly. It is not something you have to be expert at or even look good doing; you just have to know you can do it. Take a few moments and watch other skiers getting on the lift to familiarize yourself with the loading procedure. Tell the lift operator that this is your first trip so he can give you instructions on loading and unloading. Don't be embarrassed to ask him for help. He will even slow the lift down for you.

Exercises at the Top of the Hill

After standing in line for a lift and then riding it to the top of the hill, you may be cold. Certainly you will be when you are riding longer lifts later. So now is a good time to get into the habit of doing a few exercises to help you limber up and get your blood moving again. This is always important to me because I have a bad right knee; if I hurry and neglect these simple exercises, I find that when I am into my first left turn my right knee refuses to work properly and I end up making the turn virtually on one ski, which can be very dangerous.

I usually follow a pattern of five exercises:

1. Deep Breathing. Stand with your arms at your sides and, breathing through your nostrils, fill your lungs with air. Hold your breath briefly. Then force air out through your nostrils. Empty your lungs completely. Do this three times.

2. Swinging Your Arms. Do this exercise just as you did it in the room earlier in the day.

3. Circling with Your Hips. Remember to move slowly and methodically.

4. Touching Your Toes. Go down only as far as you can comfortably, stretching your leg and back muscles.

5. Half Knee Bends to the Side. Do this exercise as you did in the room but now pay particular attention to what happens with your boots and skis. The result should be automatic edging.

This series of exercises, which will take you less than two minutes, will prepare you both physically and psychologically for the hill. It will help you relax and think about the parts of your body and make it much easier for you to feel what is happening to you as you ski.

Coming Down

Before you start down the hill, review and fix clearly in your mind the body moves you will have to make in order to snowplow and turn to a stop. You have learned everything you need to know to do this with satisfactory control. Plan to practice snowplowing straight down the hill, turning and stopping all the way to the bottom.

Push off with your poles. Make a left turn and stop. Then make a right turn and stop. Work very slowly. If you have problems, stop and review. Are you following the basic steps for the snowplow and the turn? Go through them in your mind. Are you in the basic ski position? Check it. Are you relaxed? Relax.

After you have made your first run and taken the lift to the top again, pause a moment and look around you. Look at the trees and the slopes. Listen to the mountain, the silence, the way certain sounds carry. Get into the mountain, the snow, the scenery. You should realize that you are becoming part of something beautiful. I always feel skiing puts me in harmony with nature. I don't look at skiing as a way of conquering the mountain; I look at it as a way of getting close to it, of becoming a part of it. Make such stops as this a frequent and regular part of your total skiing experience.

OK, let your body relax, and start your second run. Snowplow, turn, and come to a stop; snowplow, turn, and come to a stop, all the way down the slope.

Linked Turns

On your next run down the hill, try to link two turns. To do this, turn slightly to the left, straighten back up to your central position, then make a turn to the right. Stay in the second turn until you come to a stop.

Ski a series of two or three linked turns, running straight for a few feet between each turn. Try to be smooth and rhythmical with your movements. Remember to start slowly and remain in control of your skis. Speed will come later; right now control and a sense of rhythm are most important. Go smoothly from the snowplow position into a left turn. Come out of the left turn and go smoothly into a right turn. Feel how your body and your skis work as a unit. If you get into trouble, pause on the hill and go through the whole procedure in your mind to see where you are making your mistakes. If you discover you are tense, relax.

A real sense of pleasure in skiing will come as you feel that these movements are gradually becoming automatic. Let me caution you not to exhaust yourself. Stop and rest after each run. Use this time for review. Are you putting extra effort into your weak turn? (Almost everyone has one. Mine was my left turn.) Are you standing properly on your skis? If you are tiring too rapidly, you may be squatting over your skis. Assume the basic ski position. Think about it. Relax. I know I keep harping on that word, but it is one of the keys to good skiing.

Now try to make several quick linked turns in succession. Turn only slightly out of the fall line. Weight one ski and try to steer it around, then quickly transfer your weight to the other ski and try to steer it in the other direction. Make four quick turns in this manner and then stay in your final turn to stop. They key to linking these turns quickly and efficiently is in rhythm and weight transfer.

Linked snowplow turns: end of left turn; return to center position (middle); beginning of right turn.

Once you can comfortably make six or seven turns in succession, vary the arc of the turns as follows: two long turns; three sharp, quick turns; two long, slow turns; then stop. If you are doing everything right on the long turns, where you have plenty of time to think about your movements, you should be able to make the quick turns almost automatically. You simply weight one ski and steer it around, then quickly transfer your weight to the other ski and steer it around. You may want to go back and review briefly the explanations of the snowplow turn. Weighting and edging should be simultaneous.

Practice

Your aim for this second day is to really get into skiing. You should make a number of runs down the hill, becoming completely comfortable with your skis. Let me say again that speed is the last thing you should be thinking about. Go slowly. Get things right. Practice edging by rolling your knees inward, weighting your outside ski by dropping your shoulder over it, and steering your skis by turning your feet in the direction you want to travel.

If you are having trouble, isolate your problems starting from the feet and working up. Concentrate on a single problem at a time. Work it out first in your mind. See what you are doing wrong and correct it before you move on to the next problem. Do not try to do too much too fast. Everything will come to you with time and practice.

Most people find they can turn better in one direction and they perpetuate this problem by stopping with their strong turn. If this is true for you, try to devote more effort to your weak turn. I suggest you make yourself stop with your weak turn. This will force you to use it for a purpose and will focus your attention on it. Gradually it will come up to the quality of your strong turn.

As your balance improves with more skiing and you gain greater confidence in your ability to turn and stop quickly, you will find that you can narrow the V of your skis in the snowplow and travel a little faster. But don't eliminate the V completely yet. In time, of course, you can and will, but now you need it for control.

When you feel ready, challenge yourself with more difficult runs

If you're having problems, exaggerate the correct movements of rolling your knee inward to edge the ski (right) and dropping your shoulder over the outside ski (below).

and tighter, more controlled turns. But don't try to push yourself ahead so rapidly that you are attempting runs that are too difficult for your level of proficiency. It is much better to practice on slopes suited to your skills and to work on perfecting your technique with linked turns that are smooth and well defined. By choosing runs that are above your level, you only expose yourself to needless injury and discouragement. Confidence is a key to learning quickly and you can break your confidence by trying to ski beyond your class. I would much rather see you be a little more cautious during these first few days than to see you lose your confidence by trying to progress too rapidly.

I learned this lesson the hard way. I was 18 and racing my first season in Europe. I decided to go all out right from the start. By mid-season, I'd fallen in nearly every race. Then at the last race before the World Championships, I realized that my problem was that I had lost my confidence. I knew the only way I could regain it was to ski a race without falling down, so I literally forced myself to ski that particular race more slowly and to stay on my feet. I ended up 8th in the slalom of the 1962 World Championships at Chamonix, France, and also regained confidence in my ability to ski a race without falling.

After that, one of my main objectives was to build confidence. I would always start fall training on gentle slopes with very simple slalom courses and try to establish a pattern of trouble-free runs. Then I would move on to more difficult courses and increase my speed, thus building my confidence slowly but solidly so I wouldn't be shaken by one or two bad runs. The next year I had a very successful season.

DETECTING AND CORRECTING PROBLEMS

When you are turning, the ski that is weighted and edged more is your turning ski; the other ski is the floating ski. The most common problem people have with the turn is that they keep their floating leg too stiff and thus too sharply edged, which causes the tips of their skis to cross. If you are having this problem, check first to see that you are in the basic ski position. Unless your knees are bent forward you cannot bend them sideways to roll your skis and edge or flatten them. Be sure to bend both knees enough to rest your shins against the fronts of your boots. And if you are still edging your floating ski too much try this: With your hand gently push your floating knee outward to flatten the floating ski and let it slide into the turn.

chapter four

As soon as you are awake on the third day you should again get skiing into your mind. Relax and go over everything you learned yesterday. Remember how it felt to move from the snowplow position into a left turn and then into a right turn. Review carefully all of the moves you had to make to bring about these turns. You should be able to see them all clearly in your mind. Also do the seven warm-up exercises as outlined in chapter one.

You have, after only two days on skis, learned the elementary controls of skiing. Knowing this ought to make you eager to get on your skis and take to the hill.

Today you face the challenge of a steeper and more difficult terrain. It will make skiing more demanding and will force you to concentrate on refining everything you have learned so you can

day three

maneuver with added speed and dexterity. You will learn to ski across a slope and will start to work on a more efficient way to turn on skis.

Once you are on the hill, but before you begin to ski, repeat the five limbering exercises I taught you yesterday.

TRAVERSE

The simplest and most efficient way to ski diagonally across a slope is the traverse. It represents your first departure from the idea of going straight down the hill. It is also the next step in enabling you to ski a steeper slope while still in complete control of your skis.

I should stress that the traverse position is the most important

In the traverse position, (seen here from the side), your uphill ski should lead slightly. You will find this is the natural thing to do.

position in skiing. It is the position you will be in ninety percent of the time after you've learned to make parallel turns. Your mastery of it is directly proportionate to the degree of smoothness and efficiency you'll have as you advance toward becoming an expert skier.

Traverse Position

First, practice the traverse position while standing still. Your skis should be pointing horizontally across the fall line, on their uphill edges, parallel, and three to four inches apart. Get into the basic ski position: knees forward, back slightly rounded, hands ahead and bent to keep the baskets of your poles back. Your uphill ski should lead slightly — about three or four inches; you will find that when you are on the hill this is the natural thing to do.

Since your uphill foot and ski are ahead three or four inches, your uphill knee will be ahead three or four inches. The same should be true for the uphill hip, shoulder, and hand. You will, therefore, be facing slightly downhill (fifteen to twenty degrees) from the direction your skis are heading. This is both natural and logical. You will be turning downhill, and, as I have said before, keeping your line of sight ahead will help you plan where your next turn is going to be.

To check the traverse position, place your poles across your skis just in front of your boots, then just in front of your knees, then your hips and your shoulders. The poles should make four parallel lines, all angled downhill, as you move them up your body from your feet to your shoulders.

The basic athletic position has to be modified in only two small ways to become the basic ski position for the traverse. First, because you are standing sideways with your skis across the fall line, your uphill ski will be higher; therefore, your uphill foot and knee will be

The correct positions for your feet and legs in the traverse

The traverse position as seen from the front

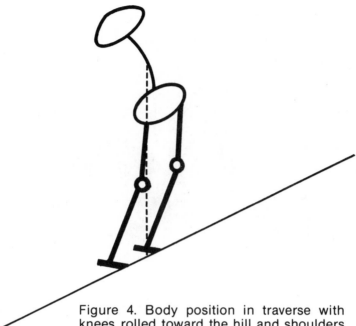

Figure 4. Body position in traverse with knees rolled toward the hill and shoulders tilted away from it

higher, and your uphill hip, hand, and shoulder should also be higher.

Second, you will need to edge and weight your skis by simultaneously rolling your knees in toward the hill and tilting your shoulders away from the hill. This will happen almost automatically; your shoulders will go out as a counter-balance when your knees move to one side or the other. Tilting your shoulders downhill will place more weight on your downhill ski. This is exactly what you want to happen.

Repeat this over to yourself: The uphill side of my body should be forward and higher than the downhill side. My knees should go in towards the hill and my shoulders should tilt downhill simultaneously.

Now that you understand the position, start across the hill in the

55

Billy Kidd traverses a slope. But he should be looking where he's going!

traverse. Point your ski tips slightly downhill to get momentum. Be sure to keep your weight forward over the balls of your feet and out over your skis. Use the snowplow to come to a stop. Turn around and cross the hill in the other direction. Pause periodically to review and digest all that is happening to you.

Whenever I'm having problems with my own technique or just preparing for difficult conditions like ice, bad visibility, or extreme steepness, I stop and check my traverse position from a standstill. And when I'm coaching aspiring young racers or members of the U.S. Ski Team or instructing beginners, I ask them to stop and do the same thing. If they are having some problem, the key to it will usually show up in their traverse.

Likewise, you should be able to tell if you are acquiring any bad habits by checking your own traverse position. Remember: Feet apart three to four inches, knees forward, hips over feet, back slightly rounded, uphill side of body (ski, foot, knee, hip, hand, shoulder) leading slightly; knees rolled into the hill, shoulders tilted away from the hill. Say it over to yourself. Fix it in your mind.

Traverse Exercises

After you feel comfortable in the traverse, try lifting the tail of your uphill ski slightly while you are gliding across the hill. This will help you get more weight on the downhill ski. Then, instead of stopping with the snow plow, try taking small uphill steps at the end of the traverse. Repeat this exercise in the opposite direction.

SIDESLIPPING

Sideslipping will teach you the sideways sliding action of your skis and how to control it with edging. Basically, you should note that when you edge your skis (by rolling your knees in toward the hill), you move forward across the hill. And when you flatten your skis (by rolling your knees away from the hill), you start to slide sideways. It is important to recognize and feel both of these sensations because they will be essential to you later when learning the parallel turn.

57

When you feel comfortable in the traverse, try taking small uphill steps to stop instead of using the snowplow.

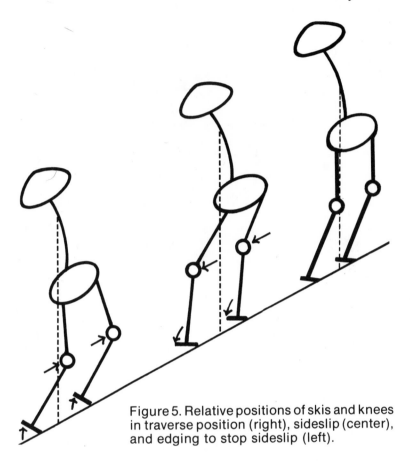

Figure 5. Relative positions of skis and knees in traverse position (right), sideslip (center), and edging to stop sideslip (left).

Practicing Sideslipping

The terrain for practicing sideslipping should be a smooth, well-packed, short slope that is slightly steeper than anything you have skied before. Stand in the traverse position, skis across the hill on their uphill edges, knees in, shoulders out. Your poles should be lifted out of the snow, with the baskets behind you.

Keep your shoulders tilted out over your skis and your knees away from the hill to decrease the edging of your skis. As your skis flatten against the snow, they should begin to slide sideways down

59

the hill. If more of your weight is on the downhill ski, as it should be, your skis will not slide out from under you; you will slide sideways on them.

To stop sliding sideways, roll your knees back into the hill and, in this way, increase the edging of your skis. It is important to keep your knees bent forward, as I stressed when talking about the basic ski position. This will give you better control when edging and flattening your skis.

If the snow is not well packed and offers resistance, or if the slope is not steep, try using your uphill pole to initiate the sideslip.

At this point it would be good for you to take a break and go over in your mind the techniques of sideslipping and edging. Remember that the most important action for initiating and controlling the sideslip is rolling your knees — away from the hill to initiate and toward the hill to control.

Billy Kidd goes from traverse position (facing page top) to side-slipping position (facing page bottom) and back to the traverse position (below)

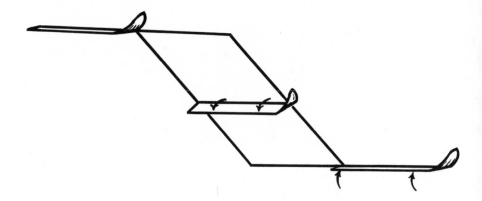

Figure 6. In the diagonal sideslip, your skis
move simultaneously forward and downhill.

The Diagonal Sideslip

To execute the diagonal sideslip, start from a running traverse.
Release the edges of your skis by rolling your knees away from the
hill, and allow your skis to slide sideways while you are moving
forward. To stop the sideways sliding, edge your skis by rolling your
knees into the hill.

Practice alternately edging and sliding while running in a traverse
until you feel you have mastered the technique. As with every skiing
exercise, you should practice the diagonal sideslip in both
directions.

A Mistake to Avoid

Be especially careful to avoid leaning or tilting your shoulders into
the hill while you are traversing or sideslipping. It is a natural
tendency to lean into the hill but it is not right. You should detect
this error early in your practice of the traverse and correct it. One of
the most difficult but important things in good skiing is keeping your
weight over your downhill ski. Remember, knees into the hill,
shoulders away from the hill.

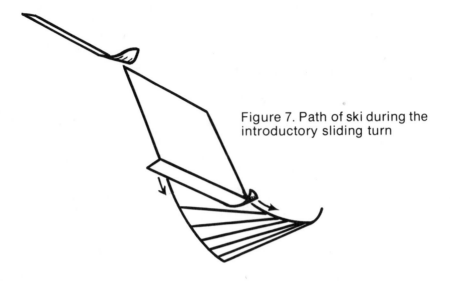

Figure 7. Path of ski during the introductory sliding turn

THE INTRODUCTORY SLIDING TURN

If, when you do the diagonal sideslip, you apply a steering action to your skis, you can make a sliding turn that will bring you to a stop.

Doing the Turn

Take the following steps:

1. Traversing across the hill, release your edges and let your skis go into a diagonal sideslip.

2. Quickly steer your skis slightly uphill by turning the tips uphill and pushing the tails downhill. Slide to a stop. You should not rotate or twist your shoulders to try and make the sliding turn. Steer your skis through the turn by simply turning or twisting your feet.

3. After gradually sliding to a stop several times, try stopping quickly by rolling your knees into the hill and edging your skis.

Now you should stop and go over in your mind the techniques of traversing, sideslipping, and edging. You should realize how important the action of your knees is to initiating and controlling your sideslip and you should be aware of the part edging plays in

63

making a sliding turn and in bringing you quickly to a stop.

Edging should get your special attention. It was always a part of ski technique I worked hardest on perfecting. At the world's biggest traditional races — the Lauberhorn at Wengen, Switzerland, the Hahenkalm at Kitzbühel, Austria, and the Olympics and the World Championships — the steep slalom courses are sprayed with water and iced until they are as hard as a skating rink. The reason for this is, of course, to prevent holes and ruts from forming so the late starters will have the same chance of winning as the early starters. Skiing on these courses is difficult and demanding. Because I always emphasized edging in my own practice, I found I could ski my best under these challenging conditions.

STEM TURN

Now you are ready to try combining a faster and smaller snowplow turn with the traverse. This will give you enough control to ski more intermediate slopes with confidence and safety.

Stem Turn Exercise

Find a smooth gentle slope. As you traverse across the slope, tilt your shoulders (exaggerate) away from the hill, putting your weight on your downhill ski, and slide your uphill ski into a small snowplow (this is called *stemming*). Then bring your skis parallel again. Repeat this all the way across the hill. Then go back in the opposite direction, opening and closing the snowplow *(stemming)* until you feel you can do it comfortably. You should not be trying for speed but for smoothness and efficiency.

You are now ready to make a stem turn. Extend the above exercise by putting more weight on your uphill ski when it is in the snowplow; this should make it turn. Maintain this snowplow turn all the way around until you come to a stop.

Traverse in the opposite direction and repeat the exercise again, making a snowplow turn and coming to a complete stop. Be sure your weight ends up over your downhill ski.

Next, with your weight on the downhill ski at the end of the turn, slide your skis parallel and traverse across the hill in the opposite

64

Billy demon-
strates the stem
turn exercise as it
would be exe-
cuted crossing a
hill from left to
right.

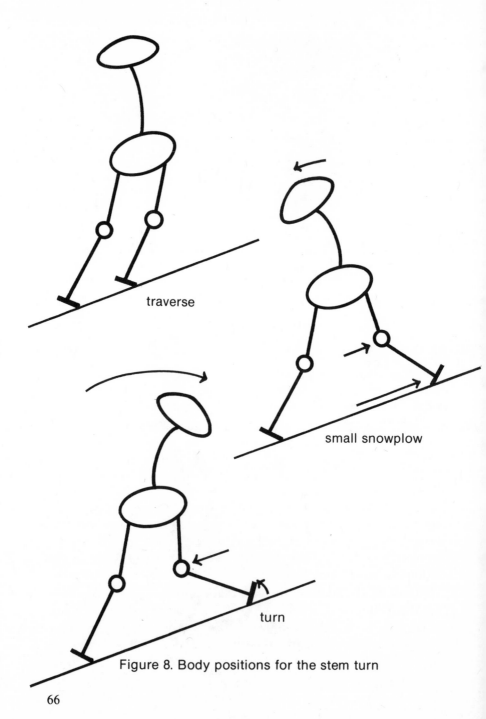

traverse

small snowplow

turn

Figure 8. Body positions for the stem turn

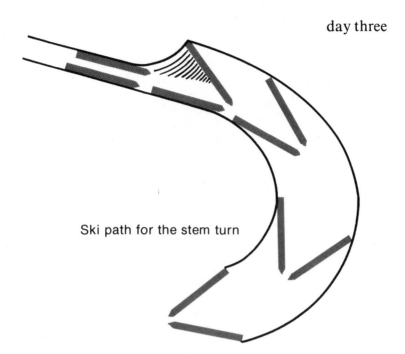

Ski path for the stem turn

direction. Repeat this and link the turns into a rhythmical pattern.

Now go back up the lift and make linked stem turns all the way to the bottom of the slope. Practice until you feel you have grasped the technique for linking up your stemmed turns.

Correcting Mistakes

If you find you're having trouble initiating the stemmed turn, it's probably because of the same basic weighting problem you had with the basic snowplow turn. Remember to roll your knee in to edge your turning ski and to drop your shoulder out over it, thereby stepping most of your weight on that ski and steering it into the turn.

If you start going too fast while linking up your turns, you are not completing the arc of your turn or ending with your skis across the fall line as they should be.

Do not be confused by the fact that the uphill, stemmed ski in your turn becomes your downhill ski at the end of your turn. Think of it as your outside ski or your turning ski, as in the snowplow turn. If you have trouble with this concept, stop and think it through until it is completely clear in your mind.

Billy Kidd does the stem turn.

68

The pole plant

Elementary Pole Plant

When you feel comfortable with the stem turn, try planting your pole in the snow just before you begin your turn. As you traverse across the hill, lift your downhill hand and plant that pole with an easy down and up motion. You should plant it downhill and ahead of you, at an angle about forty-five degrees down and forward of your feet. When you have done this, initiate your turn. The pole plant will help you a great deal as a psychological preparation for starting the turn. Just touch the snow and then ski around the spot you touched.

chapter five

By now it should be almost automatic for you to begin each morning thinking about skiing. You made your greatest advances during the first two days, when you learned the basic principles and gained initial control of your skis. From now on everything will be a matter of quality and degree. Things you have learned separately will be linked together. You will be moving toward a complete sense of a technique. Do remember the importance of going through the warm-up routine (chapter one).

As a start today, go through the previous three days' exercises in your mind. See how each exercise fits in with the next exercise. Evaluate your own progress.

Then let yourself relax for a moment. Do not think about the technical aspects of skiing. Think instead about the more esthetic and emotional things connected with skiing. How does it feel to be

day four

on the hill? Think about the mountain air, the snow. Treat yourself to a few moments of purely esthetic indulgence. You will have to give a lot of yourself to this demanding sport, but what you can take from it in return is almost immeasurable.

Skiing, for me, has been full of sensual experiences. There are things I have encountered while skiing that I'll never forget. I remember the smell of wood smoke from houses beside the trails in the Alps, the sight of black ice on a lake at ten-thousand feet in Portillo, Chile, the sound of an avalanche falling five-thousand feet on the Jungfrau in Switzerland, the startling scent as I skied through a eucalyptus forest in Australia, the suddenness with which I came upon a hundred-foot-deep crack in the ice on the side of Mont Blanc. These are only a few examples of the experiences that skiing can offer if you are open to them.

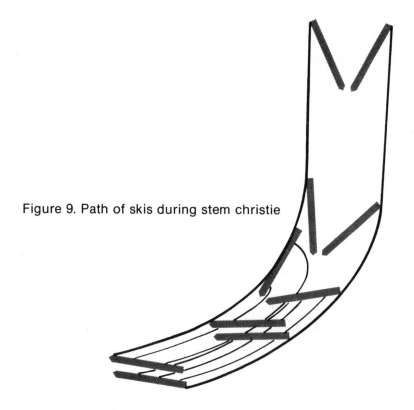

Figure 9. Path of skis during stem christie

STEM CHRISTIE

The stem christie is a higher-speed turn that will enable you to ski even steeper slopes and maintain better control of your skis. You should learn the stem christie on the same sort of smooth, gentle, well-groomed slope you were skiing yesterday.

First, go back and repeat the traverse exercise for the introductory sliding turn I introduced on day three. I ask you to do this to reacquaint you with sliding, twisting your feet to steer, and edging.

Then start down the fall line in a small snowplow. Make a right turn by edging your left ski and simultaneously weighting that ski by dropping your shoulder. As soon as your skis turn past the fall line, slide your right ski parallel to your left ski and skid to a stop. Then repeat the turn in the opposite direction.

Now link both turns with a traverse between them: Turn, traverse, turn. By finishing the turn with your skis parallel and edging increased, you will go directly into a traverse. When you can make a stemmed turn ending with parallel sliding, as you have just done, you have executed a stem christie.

Use the pole plant as a timing device to initiate your turn. Just touch the pole in and out and immediately weight your outside ski. Think about it this way: *Plant, stem, slide.* If you find it necessary to review the pole plant, return to the discussion of it on day three.

Now practice the stem christie at faster speeds. Make your turns with a quick, rhythmical shifting from side to side. Try to get it down to this simple pattern: *Step, twist, slide; step, twist, slide.* The object of this exercise is to get your reflexes working faster and to get you to transfer your weight from one ski to the other with more coordination. *You will turn faster if you plant your poles faster. Pole planting will force you to begin your next turn.*

REVIEW

At this point I suggest you take some time at the bottom of the hill to go over carefully everything you have done so far today and fix it clearly in your mind. Do this consciously and methodically, and make sure all of the above material is thoroughly understood. If you are skiing with a friend, you both can go through it together.

When you are ready, move to a steeper slope and do the exercises for the stem christie again, using a little more speed. Remember to push the tails of your skis away from you with a skidding action to execute small turns across the fall line. To stop the skidding, edge your skis at the end of the turn by rolling your knees quickly into the hill.

Practice for the rest of the day on increasingly steeper slopes. When you are comfortable with this turn, try using a smaller stem, closing your skis earlier, and pushing your tails around aggressively.

As you increase your speed, you will find that for stability you have a natural tendency to lower your center of gravity. You should do this only slightly because crouching down too much will make you unable to absorb the bumps or moguls you'll find on steeper

slopes. I learned the importance of standing upright when I was fourteen and skiing for the first time in Colorado at the Junior National Championships. The snow in Colorado is very dry, ideal for recreational skiing but difficult to pack down for racing, and the course became rutted and bumpy almost immediately. I had a habit of bending over too much from the waist, which made it impossible for my legs to absorb the bumps. I was thrown off the course and fell. Even today I have to remind myself to stand upright when I'm skiing on fast or uneven terrain.

CORRECTION AND DETECTION

Because the stem christie is a faster turn, you will have to make sure you get your weight out onto your turning ski quickly and keep that ski weighted throughout the turn. If you have trouble closing your inside ski at the fall line, you have too much weight on it. To correct this, make a conscious drop of your shoulder over the outside ski and apply more forward and inward pressure with your turning knee. It is most important to roll your knees into the hill to keep increasing the degree of edging until you have finished your turn and are ready to start turning in the opposite direction.

74

Billy Kidd does the stem christie.

chapter six

Today you should try to find a new and more interesting run. Make
it your first project of the day. Think about it as one of the pleasures
of skiing. Anticipate finding this new run, having this new
adventure. One of the many things skiing can offer you is change.
Every day the hill and the snow and the feeling of the air will be
different to you. You can catalog these changes in your mind and
predict what kind of skiing you are going to have on a given day. But
there will always be certain surprises. And these surprises will keep
skiing fresh and exhilarating for you. In order to be physically
prepared to cope with surprises, be sure you do the seven warm-up
exercises.

day five

PARALLEL TURNING

The greatest enjoyment in this sport comes from being able to ski any mountain. And the beginning of this kind of advanced skiing is parallel skiing. Once you have learned its basic technique you can spend years mastering it and trying it on every snow condition and terrain.

The parallel turn is a sophisticated turn, one to which you will progress naturally from the stem christie. To learn the parallel turn you will need to practice unweighting your skis so they'll turn easily and pivoting your skis around your feet.

Billy Kidd coming out of a parallel turn

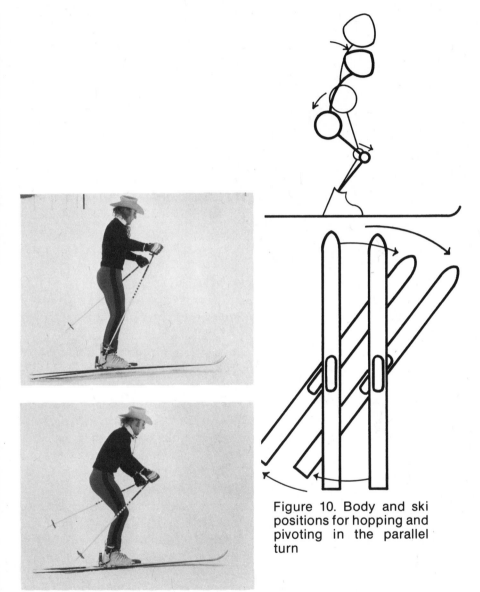

Figure 10. Body and ski positions for hopping and pivoting in the parallel turn

Hopping in preparation for pivoting in the parallel turn. Hop a couple of inches off the snow, keeping weight balanced over center of skis (top); keep knees bent and back rounded for landing (bottom).

Stationary Exercise

Standing on the flat in the basic ski position, hop and bring your skis completely up off the snow. Most of your spring should come from your knees. The tips and tails of your skis should both come up at the same time; you must, therefore, maintain your balance over the center of your skis. When you land, flex your knees to absorb the shock.

Hop again and pivot your skis slightly to the left. Your feet should be the central point of the pivot. Now hop once more and pivot your skis to the right. Link these exercises into a continuous rhythmical pattern — left, right; left, right. Try to keep your upper body still as you hop and pivot. Most of the action should be in your legs.

Next, introduce a pole plant into the exercise. Plant your left pole and immediately hop and pivot to the left. Plant your right pole and immediately hop and pivot to the right. Continue alternating your pole plant and hopping — left, right; left, right.

When coaching young racers, I use this hop and pivot exercise to promote a well balanced position in the center of the skis. To do it successfully you must bring into play two principles of the basic athletic position: To initiate the hop you must flex your knees and round your back. To be able to pivot your skis around your feet quickly you must have your weight over the balls of your feet.

When I was racing I found I could turn my skis much more quickly by using my feet as the pivot point than by using my ski tips, which was then the traditional way. I would practice quick turns by skiing a very steep run, like the National at Stowe, and trying to make a turn every three or four feet by hopping and pivoting. At the time my purpose was simply to practice the pivoting, but I soon found that this exercise was also good for practicing edging because it only gave me time to edge with my knees and not with my hips. Then I realized that it was equally good for improving the timing of my pole plant.

One final word about this exercise. It is only an exercise and you will eventually want to replace the hopping with a gentle unweighting of the skis on the upward motion, which we will discuss a little later.

Hopping with a pole plant

Moving Parallel Exercise

Find a very gentle incline and do the hopping and pivoting exercise — but while moving down the fall line. Start in a straight running position down the slope, feet about three to four inches apart. After you are moving, flex your knees, and unweight your skis with a little hop. Keep your body relaxed and forward, in the basic ski position, to avoid landing on the tails of your skis.

After practicing the hop, combine it with the pole plant. To do

81

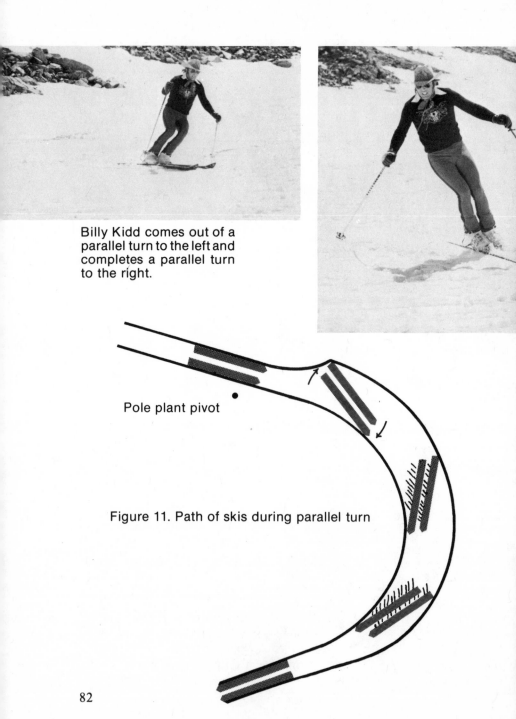

Billy Kidd comes out of a
parallel turn to the left and
completes a parallel turn
to the right.

Pole plant pivot

Figure 11. Path of skis during parallel turn

this, bring your left pole up and forward as you prepare for unweighting. Plant it and immediately hop to unweight your skis. Bend your knees to absorb the shock of landing and to prepare yourself for the next hop. Plant your right pole and hop again. Coordinate the planting of your pole with the downward motion of your body and the removal of the pole plant with the upward motion of your body. Maintain a continuous smooth rhythm.

Now introduce a pivot and skid motion with the hop. From a straight running position down the fall line, plant your left pole, hop, and pivot your skis to the left. Bend your knees when you land and edge your skis to stop the sideways sliding. Repeat this exercise to the right.

Now link the two, building a continuous pattern — plant your pole, hop, pivot and skid; plant your pole, hop, pivot and skid.

You should practice this exercise until you can make three or four turns in a row with proper balance. As you grow more comfortable with the entire exercise, you will notice you can gradually eliminate the hop. Simply unweight your skis by rising up sharply, pivoting your feet, and steering into the rest of your turn.

When you have eliminated the hop you should be able to lighten your skis without straightening up completely. Always keep a certain amount of flex in your ankles, knees, and back.

Now go to a somewhat steeper slope. (You will find that the parallel turn is much easier when you can go faster.) Work on refining the hop out of your turn completely. Try for more speed without sacrificing any of your rhythm.

When you have made a complete run, stop and think back over everything you must do to make a parallel turn. Put the movements of the turn together carefully in your mind. Visualize yourself doing them. Try to feel what each movement of your body does to the performance of your skis.

DETECTION AND CORRECTION

Let me emphasize that the jumping and hopping are not the final forms in the parallel. They simply allow you to pivot your skis more easily. Once you have learned to balance and pivot both skis equally from the center, you should just weight and unweight to make your skis light enough to pivot. Most of the action should be in your legs.

Rhythm is important in skiing; your turns should be linked smoothly. Remember to end each turn by tilting your shoulders out over your downhill ski and rolling your knees into the hill to edge your skis. This strong edging at the end of the turn will stop any sideslipping and will set you up automatically for your next turn.

MENTAL AWARENESS

As you can see, I am stressing the need for mental awareness in your learning process. This whole idea of visualizing, of putting mind over matter, was brought home to me forcefully in 1970 at the World Championships. I had strained my back badly a few weeks before and couldn't practice on the downhill course. I had only a certain amount of strength left in my back and I wanted to save it for the actual race. My solution was to go up and watch the other racers train.

But I did not sit by idly. I noted how the others skied the course, what their body positions were, and how they reacted to various turns and bumps. I memorized the course thoroughly. In fact, I can still see it: Out of the start, three sharp turns — very precise; pick up speed — sixty miles per hour across the flat; into the woods, cutting in three feet from the snow fence; a sharp S-turn; seventy miles per hour over three rolls — try to stay on the snow; left turn, right turn, very bumpy; a sharp drop-off, then a left turn over the road; right turn, then straight for the finish. I visualized how I would ski it, what it would feel like.

I took only three practice runs on the course, which was the equivalent of about a day of practice. Normally I would have practiced continuously for five days. Still, when I took my first run down the course, I felt entirely comfortable, and I had excellent training times. The result was good enough to give me a fifth in the downhill, and this, added to my performance in the slalom and giant slalom, made it possible for me to win the gold medal in the combined.

chapter seven

Before you begin your sixth day of skiing, stop and reflect on everything that has happened to you in the past five days. When you first read that I could help you learn to ski with confidence and control in six days, possibly you were skeptical. Now, however, if you have been diligent, you can look back and see that you have indeed learned the basics of good, safe skiing.

Many of you will have completed the course in less than six days. Some of you may be having a few problems in some areas. This is perfectly natural; it happens in anything you do. But nothing we have discussed should be impossible for you to master; it will only require time and concentration and honest effort on your part.

At this point, what you ought to have achieved, beyond basic balance and control, is complete confidence in your ability to master

day six

the art of skiing. Instead of looking like the beginner you were five days ago, you have assumed the smooth style of the expert. You are traveling faster and skiing the intermediate runs. Soon you can move on to the more challenging runs of the mountain. You have brought yourself to a point at which you can really anticipate all of the pleasures skiing has to offer. (By this time, the seven warm-up exercises in your room as well as the series of five exercises at the top of the hill should almost have become second nature.)

Today you will work on improving your technique. The emphasis will be on refining your parallel turn and making it more efficient. You will also try skiing the bumps for the first time. I will show you how they can make turning even easier.

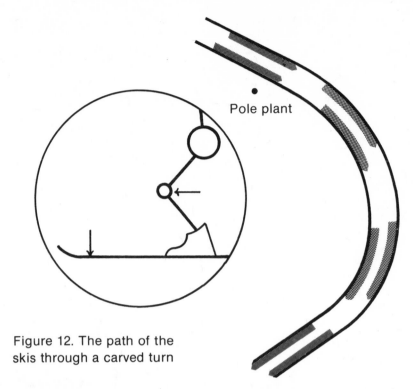

Figure 12. The path of the
skis through a carved turn

CARVING AND THE POLE PLANT

I like to describe the action of carving as a feeling you might have if your skis were turning on railroad tracks. If you look back at your tracks after a nicely carved turn, they will be very narrow, not much wider than the skis themselves. When you carve a turn, there should be very little sideslipping.

When carving you should concentrate on your ankles and knees. Bend them forcefully forward and into the turn. This applies pressure to the fronts and the edges of your skis. If you are carving correctly, your skis will turn almost automatically.

In order to combine carving with the pole plant, stand in a traverse position on the hill with your skis across the fall line. When you roll your knees into the hill notice that your shoulders almost automatically tilt away from the hill. Conversely, when you tilt your shoulders away from the hill your knees roll into the hill. So it follows that when you reach downhill to plant your pole, you pull

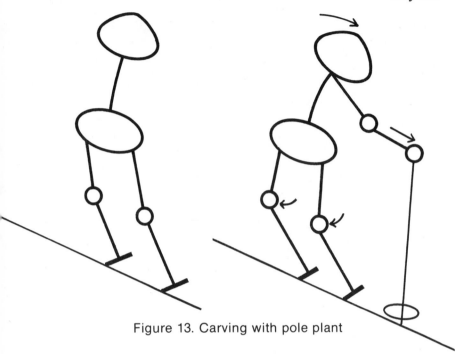

Figure 13. Carving with pole plant

your downhill shoulder down and your knees automatically roll into the hill and press forward to carve your turn.

To take the greatest advantage of the design of my skis and boots, I try to carve all my turns. Where carving a turn really feels good is on a wide, smooth intermediate trail such as Buddy's Run at Steamboat Springs, Colorado. When you really know how to carve a turn well and you are on this kind of run you discover a kind of skiing that is almost effortless and that lets you feel the character of the trail. You realize, too, that you've developed a precision and understanding that lets you be, perhaps as much as anyone ever can be, as one with the mountain. It's a fantastic feeling. I get it when I'm making long smooth turns down Buddy's Run, almost four thousand feet above the valley floor. I lose myself in that crystalline silence. There's something almost magical in hearing only the sound of my own skis. I find myself looking down over the town of Steamboat Springs, beyond it over at least one hundred miles of rolling hills to the west.

(Above and facing page) Billy Kidd carves a turn.

SKIING THE BUMPS

Most people fear skiing rough terrain, but with a little practice you can feel comfortable in the bumps. In fact, you will find that bumps can actually help you negotiate your parallel turns.

The basic rule for skiing bumps is to keep your head on the same plane at all times and let your knees absorb the sudden changes in terrain. You simply use your knees as shock absorbers.

Exercise for Skiing the Bumps

Approach a bump, traveling in the basic ski position — knees bent, back slightly rounded, hands forward. As your skis go up the front side of the bump, bend your knees and allow the bump to push your feet up, but without allowing it to change the level of your upper body and head.

After you pass the crest of the bump, push your feet back down by straightening your knees. You should once again be in the basic ski position. If you do this properly, allowing your knees to bend and straighten freely, you should maintain contact with the snow at all times. And this is the key to skiing the bumps.

(Above and facing page) When skiing over bumps, keep your head level and allow your legs to absorb the shock of the bump.

(Above and facing page) Moving exercise
to practice parallel turning over bumps

When I was racing on the professional circuit, I found that the big man-made bumps were a true test of this principle. The bumps are sometimes eight or nine feet high and suddenly drop straight off the back side. Skiing them at forty miles per hour, even using my whole body to absorb the thrust and drop, I would sometimes fly fifty feet through the air before I would regain contact with the snow. By maintaining as constant a level with my head as was possible at those speeds and under those conditions and by letting my legs take most of the force of the bumps, I could keep my skis completely under control.

Parallel Turns in the Bumps

To practice parallel turns in bumps, select a large round bump or mogul on an intermediate slope. Stand on top of the bump with only the part of the ski under your foot touching the snow. The tips and

tails of your skis should be free and clear of the snow. Now see how effortless it is for you to pivot the tips and tails around your feet. Pivot first to the left, then to the right.

Now traverse, in a fairly upright position, slowly across the hill toward the bump. As your skis go up the side of the bump, bend your knees and get ready to plant your downhill pole. When your skis reach the crest of the bump, plant your pole and pivot your feet to start your turn.

As your skis slide down past the crest of the bump, straighten your knees, move your weight forward, and gradually increase the edging of your skis. Remember to start leaning out and weighting your outside ski just as soon as it turns into the fall line. With this turn, timing is most important.

Practice your turns in the bumps until you can make them with almost no effort. If you start having trouble, stop and think through everything you should be doing. Check your traverse position. Make certain you are relaxed and that your timing is right.

DETECTION AND CORRECTION

Be sure you are relaxed. I can't emphasize that word enough. Relax! The bumps may look difficult, but with care you can ski them comfortably. If, however, you try to ski them stiffly, they will throw you off balance.

Do not sit back. Force yourself to look ahead and anticipate the bumps before you encounter them. Push your feet back down on the back sides of the bumps so that you maintain good contact with the snow.

At first when you are turning on the crest of a bump your timing may be wrong — either early or late. Don't worry. It takes practice to master this exercise. Try it more slowly several times. A lot of speed at first will make the turn extremely difficult. Once you get the feel of turning on the bumps, you'll find that you can go faster and that it adds a new dimension to your skiing.

ONE FINAL HINT

I always found it helpful to watch films of myself and other racers. In the fall especially, I would sit for hours running and rerunning (at regular speed and at slow motion) footage of various practice runs and races, noting how each skier reacted to every bump and turn on a particular course. This gave me insight into little details I didn't always remember at the time I was running a course and it also allowed me to check my technique against the techniques of other racers.

To anyone wanting to ski better I would recommend watching skiing films and television shows. If you pay attention to details, you can learn a great deal from watching expert skiers, especially racers. The reason I emphasize racers is that they ski under the most demanding conditions: They travel at speeds of up to eighty miles per hour and yet must make precise turns that cannot vary more than a few inches in either direction.

As you watch the racers, pay careful attention to the following things: feet (placed slightly apart for better balance), knee action (used for edging and flex), pole plants (done quickly and smoothly), the attitude of the upper body (kept quiet, with hands out in front and weight forward), and, finally, stance (helping the whole upper body absorb the bumps through the action of the knees and legs).

Happy Skiing!

glossary

Angulation: A body position in which the knees and hips angle into the hill while the shoulders angle away from the hill.

Avalement: The use of the knees to absorb irregularities in the terrain without changing the position of the upper body.

Bottom camber: Arc of the bottom of the ski; it helps to distribute the skier's weight evenly along the ski.

Corn snow: Spring snow that has a granulated texture caused by thawing and freezing.

Downhill: One of the three classic Alpine racing events, characterized by bumps, high-speed turns, jumps, and speeds of up to eighty-five miles per hour.

Edging: Increasing the angle between the bottom of the skis and the surface of the snow by making a lateral movement of the knees.

Fall line: The line a ball would take rolling down a hill.

FIS: International Ski Federation, the governing body of competitive skiing.

Flat light: A lighting condition that makes it difficult for a skier to see irregularities in the snow.

Flex: The stiffness of a ski, which can vary markedly from tip to tail.

Giant slalom: A race consisting of controlled high-speed turns through a series of gates.

GLM: Graduated Length Method, a method of teaching skiing by employing successively longer skis.

Gondola: An enclosed ski lift generally used for longer runs and in colder climates.

Herringbone: Climbing a hill with skis in a wide V configuration.

Jet turn: An action that occurs when the energies accumulated by a hard edge set at the end of one turn are released to propel the skier into the next turn.

Mogul: A large bump on a heavily traveled slope caused by skiers turning in the same place; moguls usually occur in series called mogul fields.

Pole plant: The action of placing the tip of the pole in the snow prior to making a turn.

Powder: New, light, dry, and unpacked snow.

PSIA: Professional Ski Instructors of America, the governing body of organized ski instruction in the United States.

Safety binding: A binding that releases the boot from the ski at a point of stress to prevent injury.

Schuss: Skiing straight down the hill.

Side camber: The variation in the width of the ski from tip to tail.

Slalom: A race consisting of a series of quick turns through closely placed gates.

100

Steering: A rotary turning of the skis with the feet.

Stemming: Stepping one ski out to initiate a turn.

"Track!": The term called out by an overtaking skier requesting the right-of-way.

Wide track: An open stance that a learning skier should use to maintain good balance.

index

A

Angulation, 97
Arm and shoulder exercises, 4, 41
Avalement, 97

B

Back exercises, 4-5
Basic ski position, 17-18, 42, 71-72,
   88-89, *illus.* 16
Beginner's techniques, 13-26
   exercises, 14-17, *illus.* 15
Bindings, 7, 25, 26, 98
Boots, fit of, 6-7
Bottom camber, 97
Breathing exercises, 2, 40
Bumps, skiing over, 88-95, *illus.* 90,
   91, 92, 93
   mogul, 98

C

Camber
   bottom, 97
   side, 98
Carving, 85-87, *illus.* 86, 87, 88, 89
Chairlift, 9, 10
Climbing side step, 21-22, *illus.* 21
Clothing, 7-8
   boots, 6-7
Conditioning. *See* Exercising
Corn snow, 97

D

Downhill racing, 97

E

Edging, 26, 28, 40, 41, 44, 55, 59,
   61, 62, 78, 98
   in turns, 32, 47, *illus.* 28
Equipment, 6-8

Etiquette, 11
Exercising, 1-6, 40-41
   beginner skier's, 14-17, *illus.* 15
   mental, 37-38, 71
   warm-up, 2-6, 41, 74

F

Fall line, 21-22, 98
Falling, 11, 25-26, 72, *illus.* 24-25
FIS, 98
Flat light, 98
Flex, 98
Foot exercises, 6

G

Gear, 6-8
Giant slalom, 98
GLM, 98
Gloves, 8
Goggles, 8
Gondola lift, 98
Graduated Length Method, 98

H

Hall, Doug, *illus.* 3
Head and neck exercises, 4
Herringbone, 98
Hip exercises, 4-5, 41
Hopping and pivoting, 75, 78, 79-
   83, *illus.* 77, 79

I

International Ski Federation (FIS),
   98

J

J-bar lift, 9-10
Jet turn, 98
Jogging, 2

K

Kidd, Billy, 37, 40, 46, 83, *illus.* 3, 34, 54, 58, 59, 63, 66, 72, 73, 74, 76, 80–81, 88, 89
Knee bend exercises, 5–6, 41
Knee bend position, 24, 25

L

Leg muscle-building exercises, 5–6, 22, 41
Lifts and tows, 8–11, 40
  rules regulating, 10–11
  types of, 8–10, 98
Linked turns, 42–44, 65, *illus.* 43

M

Mental exercises, 37–38, 71
Mittens, 8
Mogul, 98

P

Pants, 8
Parallel turn, 75–83, *illus.* 74, 76, 77, 80–81
  on bumps, 92–94, *illus.* 92, 93
Parka, 8
Physical conditioning. *See* Exercising
Passing on the slope, 11
Pivoting, 75, 78, 79–83, *illus.* 77, 79
Pole plant, 67, 71, 78, 79–82, 85–87, 98, *illus.* 67, 79, 87
  over bumps, 94
Poma lift, 9
Powder snow, 98
Professional Ski Instructors of America (PSIA), 98

R

Racing, 62, 95
  downhill, 97
  giant slalom, 98
  slalom, 98
Rental equipment, 6
Right of way, 11, 99
Rope tow, 9

S

Safety bindings. *See* Bindings

Safety straps, 11, 13, 14, *illus.* 14
Scarves, 7
Schuss, 98
Side camber, 98
Sideslipping, 55–60, *illus.* 57, 58, 59, 60
  diagonal, 60
Sidestepping, 21–22, *illus.* 21
Ski areas, 8–11
Skiing techniques. *See* Basic ski position; Beginner's techniques; Climbing side step; Sideslipping; Snowplow; Straight running; Traverse; Turning; Walking
Ski poles, 7. *See also* Pole plant
  control, 22–24
  falling, 25, 26
  sideslipping, 57
  putting on, 14, *illus.* 15
  safety on lifts, 10
Skis
  bottom camber, 97
  flex, 98
  length, 6, 98
  side camber, 98
Slalom race, 98
Sliding turns, 61–62, *illus.* 61
Snow conditions
  corn, 97
  powder, 98
Snowplow, 26–32, 35, 39, 41, 42, *illus.* 27–31, 33, 34, 38. *See also* Stemming
Socks, 7
Steering, 99
Stem christie, 70–71, 72, *illus.* 70, 72–73
Stemming, 62, 99
Stem turn, 62–67, 70–71, *illus.* 63, 64–65, 66
Stopping, 30, 61, *illus.* 56
Straight running, 22–25, 30, *illus.* 23
Sunglasses, 8
Suntan lotion, 8

T

T-bar lift, 9–10

Tows and lifts, 8–11, 40
  rules regulating, 10–11
  types of, 8–10, 98
"Track," 99
Traverse, 49–55, 70, *illus.* 50–54,
    57–59, 64
  position, 50–53
Turning techniques, 20–21, 44, 46–
    47, *illus.* 20
  carving, 85–86, *illus.* 86–89
  jet turn, 98
  linked turns, 42–44, 65, *illus.* 43
  parallel turn, 75–78, 92–94, *illus.*
    80–81, 92
  sliding turns, 61–62, *illus.* 61
  snowplow, 26, 31–32, 35, 39, 46,

    illus. 33, 35, 39
  stem christie, 70–71, *illus.* 70
  stem turn, 62–67

U

Underwear, 7

W

Walking technique, 18, *illus.* 19
Warm-up exercises, 2–6, 41, 74
Weight distribution and balance, 18,
    22, 24, 44, 60, 72, 78
Wide track, 99

Y

Yoga, 2